christmas
wishes

christmas
wishes

inspiring sentiments for the festive season

edited by tom burns

First edition for North America published in 2004
by Barron's Educational Series, Inc.

First published in 2003 for
WH Smith Limited
Greenbridge Road
Swindon SN3 3LD
by Tangent Publications, an imprint of Axis Publishing Limited.

All inquiries should be addressed to:
Barron's Educational Series, Inc.
250 Wireless Boulevard
Hauppauge, New York 11788
www.barronseduc.com

Library of Congress Catalog Card No. 2003112714

International Standard Book No. 0-7641-5760-4

Conceived and created by

Axis Publishing Limited

8c Accommodation Road

London NW11 8ED

www.axispublishing.co.uk

Creative Director: Siân Keogh

Editorial Director: Brian Burns

Production Manager: Tim Clarke

Printed and bound in China

9 8 7 6 5 4 3

about this book

Christmas Wishes brings together an inspirational selection of powerful and life-affirming phrases that in one way or another have touched people's lives during the festive season, and combines them with evocative and gently amusing animal photographs that bring out the full humor and pathos of the human condition.

Christmas is a time of joy and thanksgiving, but it's all too easy to lose sight of this in the midst of all the preparations, parties, and presents. These inspiring examples of wit and wisdom, written by real people based on their real-life experiences, enable us to regain our sense of perspective and rediscover the true meaning of Christmas. As one of the entries so aptly puts it—it's the warmth that comes to our hearts when the Christmas spirit returns again.

So here's to a happy Christmas and a healthy, prosperous, and peaceful New Year.

about the editor

Tom Burns is a writer and editor who has written for a wide range of magazines and edited more than one hundred books on subjects as diverse as games and sports, cinema, history, and health and fitness. From the hundreds of contributions that were sent to him, he selected the ones that best sum up what Christmas is all about—peace on earth, goodwill to all, and a stocking full of presents!

The perfect Christmas is a frozen land full of warmth.

There's nothing better than
snowfall outside, a good fire inside,
and good cheer and amiable
company all around.

May your days be merry and your heart be light, your holidays happy and your season bright.

May Christmas bring
friends to your side
and happiness to your
New Year.

Never choose to be alone at this
time of year—it's all about
reawakening your spirit for
the year to come.

Friends make Christmas merry!

And a nice warming
Christmas drink makes
it even merrier!

Your friendship is the nicest Christmas gift of all.

I always make sure to see
everyone I know before
Christmas, especially if I haven't
seen them for a while.

Though miles
apart, you're
in our hearts
at Christmas!

So remember to phone!

Christmas is a time when you get homesick—even when you're home.

Christmas is the only time that we sit around looking at a dead tree and eating chocolate out of our socks!

Relax now, the bird is in the oven.

Eventually, the preparation ends
and the feasting begins.

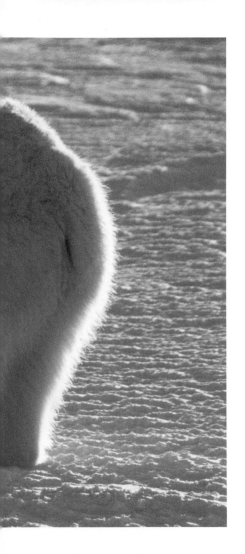

Christmas is not a time or a season, but a state of mind.

I can even think my way into
a Christmas mood at any time
of the year and it always helps
to cheer me up.

Until you feel the spirit
of Christmas, there is
no Christmas.

That's why I like to start feeling it
around mid-November.

There is no ideal Christmas,
only the Christmas you decide
to make as a reflection
of your values, desires,
affections, and traditions.

There has been only one Christmas—the rest are anniversaries.

But that's okay by me because you can never have too many anniversaries.

Christmas began in the heart of God.

It is complete only when it reaches the heart of man.

Even if it's only for five minutes,
put a little time aside to
remember what it's all about.

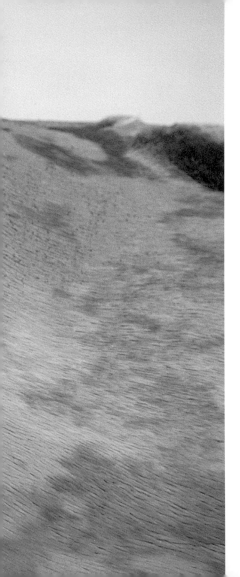

It's the warmth
that comes to our
hearts when the
Christmas spirit
returns again.

Christmas waves a magic wand over the world, and everything is softer and more beautiful.

None of us should ever forget that we need to hold on to some magic in our lives.

Perhaps the best Yuletide decoration is being wreathed in smiles.

Think about it—during the festive season, you smile at complete strangers in a way that you would not normally do, and it makes you feel so good. Why don't you do it more often?

All I want for
Christmas is my
two front teeth.

The sparkle in a child's eyes shines brighter than any Christmas lights.

It is true that Christmas is really
for kids, but that doesn't mean
you can't be a kid for that day.

Don't worry about
the size of your
Christmas tree.

In the eyes of children,
they are all 30 feet tall.

Children, Christmas is not a date.
It is a state of mind.

There's nothing sadder in this world than to wake up on Christmas morning and not be a child.

So go on—be one!

The magic of
Christmas is that
we all become
children again.

Christmas is for
children of all ages.

This Christmas, with
quietness of mind,
let us always be patient
and kind.

I find it's a good time of year to
forgive and forget, put things
behind me, and start afresh.

Put your shoes by your bed on Christmas Eve to prevent the family quarreling.

On Christmas Eve, all animals can speak. However, it is bad luck to test this superstition.

Good luck will come to the home where a fire is kept burning throughout the Christmas season.

And I shouldn't have to tell you that the fire burns brightest in your heart.

What I don't like about office Christmas parties is looking for a job the next day.

Why is Christmas just like a day at the office?

You do all the work and the fat guy with the suit gets all the credit.

There was a time when
I was younger that I didn't
believe in Santa Claus…

Now I know that
Santa Claus exists.

When you stop believing in Santa Claus, you get underwear for Christmas.

You know you're getting old when Santa starts looking younger.

Then again, when you've reached that age, you can do a lot worse than being fat and jolly...

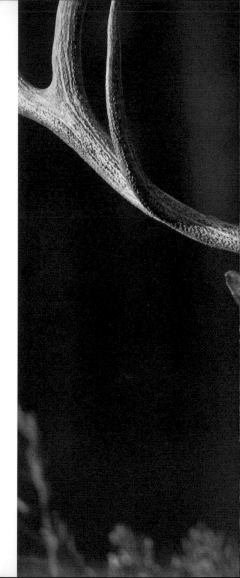

Be naughty—save
Santa a trip!

What do you call
people who are afraid of
Santa Claus?

Claustrophobic.

All together now…
quack, quack!

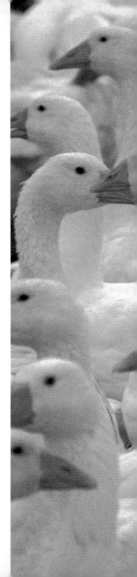

Why does Scrooge love Rudolph
the Red-Nosed Reindeer?

Because every buck is
dear to him.

Christmas is a time
when kids tell Santa
what they want and
their parents pay for it.

Much like the rest of the year,
except for the Santa bit.

I bought my kids a set of batteries for Christmas…

with a note on them saying, toys not included.

Give books for Christmas. They're never fattening, seldom sinful, and permanently personal.

Make reading a delight for children at Christmas and it will be a habit for life.

Christmas is a time when everybody wants the past forgotten and the present remembered.

There is always somebody that one is afraid not to give a Christmas present to.

Blessed are those who can give without remembering, and take without forgetting.

As a child, I'll be honest, I never could understand the idea that it was better to give than to receive. But to understand this—truly in your heart—means you've come a long way in life.

You might as well
do your Christmas
hinting early.

Even before Christmas has said "Hello," it's saying "Buy Buy."

Christmas is a race to see
which gives out first—
your money or your feet.

A Christmas shopper's complaint is one of longstanding.

Ask yourself—unless it's likely to break a child's heart, break off an engagement, or break up a marriage, is it really worth it?

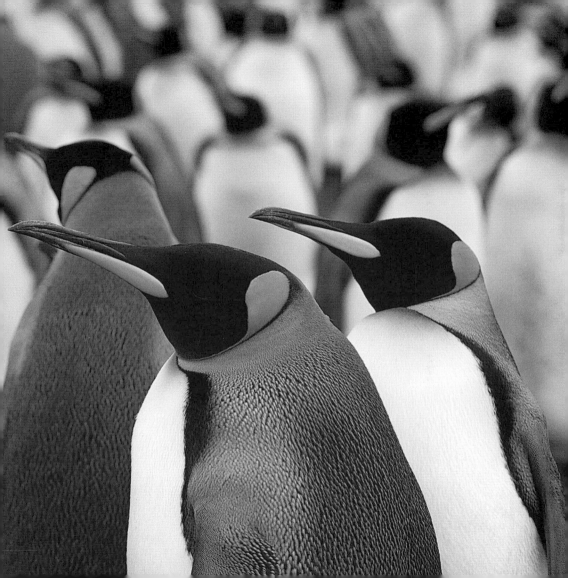

Many banks have a new
kind of Christmas club
in operation.

It helps you save money
to pay for last year's gifts.

Bah…humbug!

If there is no joyous way to give a festive gift, give love away.

It's the one sure way it will bounce back.

Remember,
love weighs more
than gold.

It is love in the heart that puts Christmas in the air.

Love is what you hear on
Christmas morning,
when you stop opening
presents and listen.

It is the sound of a child
running around the room,
squealing with delight.

You don't need Christmas
in your hands…

when you have Christmas
in your heart.

If you don't have
Christmas in
your heart, you
will never find
it under a tree.

And, for that matter, you cannot
leave it under the tree for anyone
else to find.

To cherish peace and goodwill is to have the real spirit of Christmas.

Next to a circus, nothing packs up and wears out faster than the Christmas spirit.

If only we could put Christmas spirit in jars and open one every month.

I will honor Christmas in
my heart, and try to
keep it all year.

Of course this isn't easy—but
truly good things are rarely easy.

Christmas ain't over 'til the fat angel sings!

So join in—for there is nothing
like a Christmas song to clear
your head, warm your heart,
and lift your spirit.

May peace be your gift at
Christmas and your blessing
all year through!